Retirement

Myths, Temperaments and Finances

A skinny book about potentially
the best time in your life

J. D. Stewart

To Jimmy, may your retirement be wonderful.

Cover photo provided by iStock.com
(# 16890516). All advice is to be taken in a
general and not a specific form for action.

ISBN 13: 978-1500559342
ISBN 10: 1500559342

Table of Contents

Introduction

I.   Myth I: Travel

II.   Myth II: Hobbies

III.   Myth III: Volunteering

IV.   Myth IV: Easy Life

V.   Temperaments

VI.   Worse Case Scenario

VII.   Reprogramming

VIII.   Day to Day

IX.   Finances

Conclusion

Preface

This very small book came about as a result of me talking one early morning with my greens grocer about retirement. He commented that I was here very early each week. I had arrived before any cilantro had been placed on the shelves and one of his assistance was checking to see if they had cilantro in the back of he store. As we conversed it came up that I was retired, hence my early arrival on Monday morning each week. Jimmy said it must be a great life being retired. I told him in no uncertain terms that it was one of the great trials of my life, but I had found writing to give me some direction, structure imposed upon a life without work. Unfortunately for his sake, I continued to berate the pitfalls of this final phase of my life. He got a concerned look on his face and continued to ask questions. He finally added, as I moved to the checkout counter, that I needed to write a book about the trials of and negotiable paths to retirement. I told him I might, if I did, I would give him a copy, He got his wish, this is the book and it is dedicated to him.

This book is divided into myths about retirement and the way that different people will adjust to it according to their particular temperaments and their ability to find positive aspects of this last phase of their lives. The purpose of this book is to prepare those thinking about retirement for the shock of leaving the workforce. Some will transition easily and find everyday a blessing from heaven, but some will find it anything but joyful. Temperament will determine how wonderful retirement will be. The problem is that if you turn out to be in the latter group of retirees, you will have to make some very significant changes in your life and the way you view life in general. Some people are slow and orderly others are type A personalities and have pushed and shoved their way through each work day, and suddenly find themselves out of their element. This book is an attempt to find a way for these people and those that find it less of a desperate time to cope, view each day with purpose and plan for a time of potential financial challenges.

Introduction

My retirement was very difficult. My wife told me that she wanted me to retire. She had been retired for several years and she wanted me to join her. She had taught elementary school in the public system and was perfectly matched for it and it showed. She looked twenty years younger than her age. She loved it but the changes in the schools, mostly bureaucratic changes, had made her want to get out. She retired at thirty years and after six months of rest and relaxation she began over a dozen years working several days a week at our church teaching for Mothers' Day Out.

Her transition from public teaching to retirement was easy for her. She loved the free time to do what she wanted, when she wanted, but she was retiring from a system that had gone terribly wrong. It was dumbing down everything and allowing children to run the school. Retirement for her with her situation, and not in the least her temperament, allowed her to enter partial retirement with relative ease.

In contrast, a neighbor of mine had been retired for several years, also before my time, and things did not go as swimmingly. He had hobbies, was an expert in American antiques and collectibles and was one of the evaluators when the Antique Roadshow came to town. He would rise every weekday very early and meet friends for breakfast and a chat. Everything seemed to be fine as it was with my wife until I had retired and my friend told me that his experience was not at all easy for him either. Yet he wanted to retire, had plenty of activities to occupy him and could travel when he wished. On the outside everything looked perfect.

About six months after my retirement, I was questioning who I was. There had never been any thought that I was what I had done for so many years, but it was hard for me to know who I was without the work that had, as I finally realized, been a major part of my identity. I cried and was feeling very shaky about my self and who I was. I told my retired friend how hard it was for me, and asked how he managed to prevent self doubts from affecting his time out to pasture. He told me it was a terrible transition for him, which he had hinted at before, and that everyday for the first few years he would go out into his garage workshop and cry. I did not take him to task about this hiding of his experience, but thought, why did you not tell me? Why did you not prepare me for this, one of the biggest changes in my life?

It was not that my friend wanted me to suffer and feel depressingly out of my element without the least little bit of information about his experience to guard my transition, it was hard for him to expose this part of himself.

Maybe this lack of transparency was a typically male thing. Men, it is well accepted, do not show their weaknesses as freely. My friend's reluctance, I don't know, probably could be attributed to man's ancient need to appear strong for a sign of weakness makes him look vulnerable and easy prey for others to capitalize on. Not that others would take advantage, but it may be an automatic reaction that we may not be able to consciously control.

The real concern I have for those that are about to enter retirement has more to do with their temperament, their personalities and dispositions. My wife's transition to retirement was quite positive, but her personality was easy and not the servant of the clock, in stark contrast to my anal retentiveness and the ticking second hand that had ruled my life for so long. I am not suggesting that if you are an A type personality like me that you will never adjust to being a non-worker, since you are driven by schedules and deadline. I am saying that the way you will realize the effect that retirement will have on your mental and emotional stability will have to do more with your ability to adjust to the changes in your new life.

Yes, my daydreams of my wife and I skipping across rolling hills on a cool sun shining day as the fall leaves crackled beneath our feet, was nothing like what I immediately experienced. The myths that I had come to expect to help me navigate this period in my life were never helpful and only served to confuse my understanding of what had actually happened to me in my transition from the work place.

I had to dispel the myths and based on my natural temperament for relaxation and low key living, there had to be some compromise and a major reality check. I had to get to the point, not that I wanted to, but to the point that if I went out and bought a gallon of milk that that was a pretty good day's work in retirement.

With this attitude, while dispelling the myths and misinformation, it turned out that I began to carve out a life that I found rewarding and worthy of my living it in relative ease of mind and body. With the proper planning you too can enjoy those years of retirement for which you have been waiting and avoid the downsides of retirement: myths, inflexible temperaments and failed financial issues.

I

Myth I: Travel

I know of a person who retired and spent years traveling around the world. A lavish lifestyle and very deep pockets allowed this flirtation with travel. This is great if you can manage it, but most people do not have this kind of money, and, to be quite honest, the most comfortable place for those of advancing age, as most retirees are, is at home where you can prop your feet up, lean back and vegetate on the television, which is not only more comfortable than a coach plane seat, more predictable than the inconvenience of foreign travel and a lot less expensive than a grand tour of the world.

I was told stories, myths, about couples freed from the nest of children that held them back from their sojourns, that bought a motorhome and traveled for years. One couple so desperate for the life of itchy feet and cramped accommodations, followed a football team around the states. The couple had no more interest in the college than the ball team, and little more than casual knowledge of the college, certainly no more than anyone else who never attended there.

I would like to think that all retirement travel is the result of an insatiable desire to learn about distance lands and cultures and does not amount in time to little more than photo albums of places one's friends have not visited, and the stock answer to the visitation of friends on a weeknight dinner engagement: What shall we do now? Oh, let us show you the pictures of our trip to one of the places to which you cannot afford to travel."

I must admit to being a relatively sedentary person now: one who does not like travel, and because of infirmities has not done the requisite number of journey's in recent years to family, but, what I believe to be a perfectly justifiable position, each retiree has the obligation to oneself and one's mate and other family members in finding a lifestyle and practicing it to accommodate each needy partner and their future caregivers for their years of possible and progressive infirmity. Rushing ahead to tour for extended periods of time is tantamount to a denial, that life will spare them from the ravages of time and debilitation.

Another friend has a retired relative to which my friend attends on a daily basis at great inconvenience. My friend is a dear sweet person whose relation, although greatly reduced in capacity, refuses to move closer to my friend to make the job of care much easier. This person solicits help does not travel but makes everyone that provides care travel many miles at great expense of time and energy and stands firm on his invalid independence and does little to accommodate his care givers.

Retirees must not get hung up on this dream of being footloose and fancy free, since no matter how much one travels or dreams of traveling, you must eventually come home. At home, not on a plane or a tour boat, one must find the life that exists after working for many years. Sometime people see travel as the antidote for work, even when they are still in the workforce, only to find that as they get older they are more adversely affected by the shear tiring work of vacationing. Some retirees decide that they will travel all the time to see the kids and grandkids. This is no less selfish than the man who would not move closer to his care givers. Modern times have children making a life for themselves pursuing a job or a career, and the diaspora of children seems to be, for some grandparents, spread inconveniently across the globe. Chasing these children and grandchildren around the world is not good for you nor your children's children. They need a life. I had a friend that retired and went to live in a small trailer in order to be where her daughter and her new grand baby lived. I warned her that this would not be good for her family. Since that trailer would be seen as either an unconscionable accommodation for one's mother or an embarrassment, and the daughter might suggest under situational duress that the grandmother move in with them which would be fine for the grandmother but more likely a burden on the new family.

No matter the reason for travel, this seems for most retirees something to do in an early phase of retirement if so inclined. As health issues, money and other considerations of age become a higher priority and as the inconvenience of travel becomes a greater difficulty, home most often becomes the wiser alternative.

II

Myth II: Hobbies

Fishing for an acquaintance of mine is the way he would spend all of his retirement time. It is relaxing after work and on days off, so why not a great thing to do in retirement? Fishing is a hobby that can be enjoyed any time and at any time of life, and there will be those that enjoy it the whole of their lives, but for most people fishing may lose its appeal when that becomes the sole activity in retirement. I had fantasized that I would run everyday of my retirement. This did not happen because I developed a condition before I retired that kept me from doing what I loved. Gardening was another passion that was soon to be curtailed by this condition. My friend that cried and did not tell me of his loss of retiring was crying in the center of the workshop where he had hoped to spend many joyous hours doing what he long to be doing everyday that he was at work.

Hobbies are going to be a supplement to the loss of full time employment, not a substitute for most people. It is interesting that the very origin of the concept of a hobbies is like the horse of the same name, the bobbie horse, it never goes anywhere but bounces or maybe rocks in place. Whereas a life time of work was to carry you to the comfort of reduced stress and sleeping latter in retirement, the work that you did had direction. It took you to a level of existence where you were respected for your contribution in the work place, and for the people that worked with you, those that profited from your contribution. You were not only not bouncing or rocking in place, you were not alone and laboring in a vacuum. Work can be meaningful where hobbies more often, especially when entered in on alone, may often merely structure time. That is not a totally bad thing. I have often used hobbies to structure time, but do not rely on them to fulfill me as my vocation once did. Even hobbies that involve others are not the same as one's work which often coordinated efforts that provided a living for you and possibly others in the same community awarding each involved individual value that was reinforced among others as a testimony to meaningful purpose and living.

I had a friend who spent so much time on his hobbies that he critically reduced his activity levels to the point that he suffered a heart attack. He was obsessed with his wood shop and was a very talented furniture maker in his retirement. His wife told him that he needed exercise and he was not getting it doing what he loved without consideration of his health. He became less of a hobby person and more of a healthy exerciser and lived over two more decades balancing his passionate love of woodworking and physical activity. He had not recognized that the very pastime he loved so much, that he found time for in between work schedules, resulted in a relative reduction in daily exertion, physical activity, leaving him vulnerable to heart failure.

Not everyone will experience health issue until many years after retirement, but you must not let the physical activity wane in your years after work. President Reagan chopped wood for his physical activity. There are not many young people who could endure this difficult workout. Reagan lived well into his nineties having not backed off of his exercise regimens.

Many retirees do not last long after a lifetime of work. They die within a few years. Some succumb to cancer and other diseases more genetic in nature that may not have been considered as a possible obstacle from your family history. Consider, no matter the inclination to not think of your final years, that you may need to make your hobbies a part of your bucket list. If your are leaving behind a wife or children that will have to dispose of your hobbies along with your home, cars, boats and so on, make it easy for them, to get rid of these items. Make this resolution: I will not burden my loved ones with work following my death. Instead I will dispose of my toys before I die, so they will not have to. The moment you lose interest in your hobbies get rid of them. The moment you realize that you will not be able to use the boat get rid of it and, as much as possible settle your earthly account to manageable levels. Remember hobbies go no where, but consideration of your loved ones before you leave this earth is a measure of love.

III

Myth III: Volunteering

Once week-long work is over for most, the idea of volunteering to help at some charitable institution or to help friends with their business is one way that retirees may shore up the structure that has been lost. This action may not be a direct answer for help but a deep concern that there must be something to fill the void that leaving work has created. For some this will add hours of structure into life, but for those who are still wanting to spend more time with hobbies, the same desire to have more time to yourself may be stronger than the honest drive to help others, at least at some large to moderate commitment in time and energy. My experience has been to prepare for the inevitable: expect an early morning phone call from someone who needs help. I am glad to help if I can, but do not treat the request like the duty of work. If you are not rested, not well or suffering from some compromising injury or lameness, do not give your help. You are now among those that are going to probably get up everyday with some problem, to say yes to a request to help someone requires that you be able to give them your full attention, and if your physical condition is compromised that day, you should decline or offer to help at some later date or in some other way.

There will be retirees that gravitate from volunteering time back to working part time or full time, some out of financial need and others in order to have a more demanding time filler, one with responsibility and authority. I have known those that went back to work to start a charity to raise funds for the needy. This is quite admirable, but at some time many retirees will begin to think about the obligations to family and the waning physical condition that may have brought distinct and noticeable loss of physical abilities which may only become noticeable after some new volunteer work has been agreed to. The new volunteer work or part time work may not require the same high efficiency work management in your career job or provide the remuneration that the job held for a lifetime may have provided. New work, for money or volunteerism, requires that one be able to work harder until one realizes how to work more effectively under the demands of short orders while keeping the broader view of the job under control. This is probably what you did in your career work, but now you must work and take rest breaks that may have once been an option but now may be more of a necessity. You are older and will get older; do not let it become a health robbing charitable duty or insufficient money for a overly taxing job. I have known those that have taken up a new career, when retired only to be trapped in a job that did not offer time to recover from the day's work. The work, then day to day, may become a chore and at your age you are not able to recover as rapidly from overwork as you did when you were younger. Pushing yourself may lead to a down turn in your energy level and quite possibly your health.

One of the most often missed aspects of working all day long five or six days a week for almost a full year with limited vacation time every year is the loss of structure in one's life. Even the weekends placed structure in your life. You may not find retirement with unstructured time as great as you may have imagined it. When the phone rings for help or just for talking, some of this time is filled, but phone calls and short trips will not fill the forty hour's schedule you once had. You may still be thinking I must find something to fill my day. Do not make volunteering or part time work the automatic answers to the problem of so much time on your hands. Helping others with the intention of making a schedule for yourself will not be that satisfying, and even the potential for helping others can be degraded as you, within the volunteer work, start looking for needed time for yourself. Taking away from the charitable work, say, to find a little time for yourself may not be a good message to your charity bosses. To not give yourself adequate time off may affect the love and concern with which you do your volunteering. Do not let the time that your need to yourself downgrade the contribution that you may have promised to others.

Remember that as a retired person you will be the one that people will go to first. You may not be a person that can claim a job commitment by which you pay your bills, and this leaves you open to short term commitments that may become very regular in the call from others. Helping once, whether you are able physically or emotionally may be seen as a chance for you to make a long term commitment to help, regularly helping and with time you may be tasked with taking greater and greater responsibility. It may be that the best way that you can help others is on your own where you can control your emotional and time commitment. Be careful or you might become so involved in a volunteer effort that you become the effort not meaning to commit so heavily. You may become the major player in the effort to help in some way. After all you have all that spare time.

If you think that you will need to work to support your retirement carefully consider this: you will probably never make the salary level you had in your real job, the job of many years. Do not retire until you have figured out how to make enough money to live ten to thirty or more years, years with inflation that may climb to ten time the inflation rate of your retirement year. More on finance later in the book.

IV

Myth IV: An Easy Life

For most retirees life will not be simple and for some not so easy. Both financial concerns and concerns about health arise all too often. The estimate of life after retirement is confusing. Some say somewhere between one and forty years, some same the average is only about eighteen months while other claim that a retiree, on average will die within 10 years of giving up their life's work.

Most seem to think that the lack of activity may account for the shorter lives and daily activity of the more physically capable may be the reason for suggesting the upper range of forty years. But one thing is for certain there is no absolute way of determining how long you will live. You may be fit and exercise everyday and die of some malady like cancer which may not be influenced particularly by fitness. By the time you retire, you may find you know people who have lived to the extent given by all three of these life limit statistics. But, if you do get sick or develop some disease for which you will not be able to take care of yourself, not only will your life not be easy but neither will your loved ones' lives, the ones that must take care of you.

When my step father was very ill and my mother was his care taker, they moved into a house next to us that became available because the occupant was older, had no one to take care of her and had to go to a home. A few months after the move into the neighborhood my step father died. And we were so fortunate that my mother had moved so close. Several years later my mother had a stroke, we were out of town but the neighbors knew her, saw that there was a problem and intervened until we could drive the two-hundred miles back home. Her last couple of years were less than easy for her. She had another stroke and never bounced back and within a year she was dead. Those last months of her life were physically and emotionally hard on her, but to my wife and I, even though she was conveniently next door to us, it was very, very hard. Providing care while we were at work was expensive and the daily work of keeping up with her and her needs exhausted us. We were fortunate that my mother was next door, and, unlike my friend's father who lived so far away, we had no stress and time constraints placed on us because of daily travel.

The examples that I know of and possibly you know of do not make retirement seem so joyous to those who may ultimately have to care for you. You stopped the stress of year-round work thinking that issues of health which you hoped would allow you to take better care of yourself and to embark on your remaining years for easy living, but you and I are subject to parental inheritance. Think of the problems your parents had or may now be having. Some of those maladies may show up in your retiree years or even additional problems. There is no escaping inherited disabilities or predisposition to disorders that might plague you. Had we known and could we have been able, despite the fact that we loved our parents, we may have wished in jest to have chosen our parents more carefully so that we could be without the physical problems that we may ultimately be facing. Of course this is an impossible choice, but were it possible we might have had potentially more good years and time to do the things we might have accomplished over a long and easy retirement.

Assuming that everything health wise works out for you and you live a long time, there is still the fact that the ease of life is determined also by your ability to do what you want when you want. Depending on the number of friends that you have, how dependent they are on you and how committed to them and their lives you are, you may not be able to manage a pastime of uninterrupted planned activity. When the phone rings any day your life may be different that day. This has not been bad for me, for my friends I hope know that if they need something, that I am willing to help any way that I can. I know that what I have planned for most days is only a suggestion and may not be possible.

There are so many unplanned events that have crept into my daily retirement schedule that I have a schedule that begins early and allows me time to do what I have to do before my schedule, without warning, changes on me.

Help your friends, do what you want to do but keep time open for the unexpected. Keep up with your health, have regular doctor's appointments and make sure that you plan at least one major event a week to keep you active and connected with the society which gave you direction and pushed you to contribute and give back.

V

Temperaments

No one knows exactly how they will get on in retirement. There are to many unknowns. One clue to the way you will handle this major change in your lifestyle, however, may be how you handle life in general. Do you take everything that happens in stride whether events and situations are good or bad? If you do then you will probably do better in retirement than much of my negativity has suggested. Positive people seem to have a talent for seeing most adverse situations as temporary and go about their days in a cheerful and expectant manner. These people may even have a healthier time of it.

My wife entered retirement at a relatively young age looking quite young and being very healthy. Since she taught in the public system taking all the students she was given it was to me remarkable that she could handle the pressure without it telling in her personality or her physical demeanor. She had the ability to put aside those issues that tended to sidetrack work by returning home each day from elementary school with an anticipation of the promise of the night leaving all that had been concerning at the school. This ability was to reduce her stress level tremendously. Because this was part of her temperament she carried that attitude over into retirement and had little to no problem making the transition from work to a more leisurely life. If you have this type of sanguine personality then you will probably have a better shot at your retirement years being a positive experience. This may even transfer into a healthy retirement for certainly there is a mental and emotional factor in our health in the way we adjust to life and its challenges.

In contrast, the type A personality, which better describes me and those who have what appears to be a perpetual challenge from everything that is confronted, will probably find retirement more tiring and exhausting, feeling that there is less control over life. This lack of control is a problem that festers and grows in your hopes of making everything the way you want it. If you are this type of person, then you have probably had a lifetime of directing others and trying to change the casual way in which most people, with which you interacted, conducted their affairs and help you with yours.

Life in retirement will not change these concerns. You will be embarking on a long journey in which the world will not change but you will need to enter into a state in which you must change. Shortly after my type-A breakdown six months after retirement I asked my brother who had retired fifteen years before me how he had managed it. He said that it was what appeared to be an impossible task at first, but he had finally met the challenge of retirement with a personality that was in many regards unsatisfied with the new life. He said that he had gotten to the point in his life that if he had to go out and get a gallon of milk in the morning, then that was a pretty good day's work. This was what I was challenged to attain: a life in which there were not overarching commitments to do anything, if it was not absolutely necessary. I did not have to do everything in one day or one week for that matter. This made good sense as there were people that needed my company and counsel and would best be served if I were refreshed and rested instead of filling every moment of my life with tasks for the sake of saying that I was a meticulously responsible person and being worn out by the many petty activities of life.

No one will know their ability to put up with retirement until they try it. The first few to six months may result, as it did with me, in a breakdown or it may take you longer, if you are to see trouble. And speaking now to those that have that driven personality, there is a way out of the depression and lack of identity that you may be feeling. Let us look at a worse case scenario and try and find an approach that could help you.

VI

Worst Case Scenario

So how bad can retirement get? Many people think that they will be alright because they have always been alright, but there are difficulties and pitfalls that can take a good retirement and turn it into a nightmare. Of course there are health problems. At the first indication that you will not be able to help yourself completely get your affairs in order so that someone else will not be burdened for your lack of planning for the worst. Don't hold out for your independence, it may be too late for that and do not make your caretakers, who may be older themselves, harm their health on your behalf, taking care of a selfish and an aged person.

Health problem are potentially one of the worst situations into which a retiree can fall. But there is also the matter of money which can turn a few good years into a horror story. Without sufficient funds to get you through your last years, life can be terrible. When there are also health problems there may be no solution to the retirement puzzle.

If you try to live the same lifestyle that you did when you were working: living in the same large house, keeping the same expenditures and driving the same large expensive cars, then you may be on the way to a retirement for which you cannot pay. Money commitments to your children or grandchildren may have to go by the way. Tell your children that you cannot afford the gifts or payments into their children's college fund. Not only do you need to be frugal but you also need to be honest with your loved ones about your penury condition. Let them know that you are relinquishing to them responsibilities that you cannot continue to honor.

If the difficulties of retirement have left you unable to support yourself and you are still capable of work, then by all means get a job. Part time may be a good possibility as you can probably provide your own insurance, a major concern for employers hiring help.

Cars have to be repaired. It has been said that the cheapest car you will ever own is the one you own now. Almost always a repair, usually no matter how expensive, is preferable to making a large payment each month for years when buying a new car. Keep the old one until and if your money situation clears up and you can comfortably buy a new or used car.

Try not, in the face of waning funds, to skimp on the electric bill especially if you live in the north where the cold is extreme or the south where the heat is extreme. Each year many older citizens die from exposure to the harsh elements of the weather. Under extreme weather conditions air conditioning and heating are a necessity. Do not try to skimp on environmental safety. Set aside money for the increase in utility costs for these times of extreme weather. If you cannot come up with the funds then make arrangement to be elsewhere or under someone else's roof who can afford appropriate environmental controls.

When health problems arise they are usually not overcome as they were when you were younger. Try and stay fit against wasting disorders that leave you sedentary and prone to heart trouble and stroke. If you have such problems in your family there is a chance that you will also be a victim. Stay active. Walk a little bit every day. Do not join a gym for many older people have hurt themselves setting them back unable to maintain fitness and opening themselves up to sedentary diseases. Get some light weights and work out on your own in your own home.

There will be ways to make up for a sparsity of money, reduced physical activity and adjustments to your vows of gifting. Be honest with your children, let them know of your problems and let them help you. You may be around longer so give them some of the responsibility for your care when you are not able to completely help yourself.

VII

Reprogramming

For the moment let us assume that your health is quite manageable and you have enough money and a plan for keeping you funded for the rest of your life (more on finances later). The real problem for the A-type maybe every hour of the day not holding enough challenges to make life interesting. What do you do to learn to enjoy your leisure? The first thing to do is to set up a basic schedule of required activities. These may not even be those that you want to do but must do. With the framework of the day planned then start inserting into your schedule those things that you do like and are interested in. This way you are encouraged to meet each day with not only interest but the responsible attitude that will not avoid doing the necessities. Your schedule may involve fishing and working puzzles but paying the bills on time, paying the water and electricity bill and so on, must be put ahead of, say, taking a long weekend or a vacation that will drain the bank account. In fact, you should never do anything that gets you that close to having little to no money. It may seem that buying what you want and enjoying it when you want is part of retirement, but vacations and impulsive buying have a way of draining your finances. As you will find out, retirement is more expensive, since you have forty or more hours a week to do things that cause you to spend more money.

So what about the level of activity. Find things that you can do that do not require large expenditures of money. These may not be your favorites activities, but you still need to stay within your budget so give yourself some cheap thrills as a fallback.

You may have had a pretty tight schedule while you were working so start a new one. You may even want to write it down or keep a calendar to keep up with appointments: the doctor, grocery shopping and group activities. One thing that you must get use to is the loss of memory. Most find that names and dates leave them first. Using a calendar or written schedule will help you keep up with people and events. It is good to impose a schedule on yourself. It will force you to get up and out when you get stuck in the "lazies." My wife understood this, because she is in better health and knows the advantage to being active better than I claim to know. She gave me several tasks to do like taking the garbage and recyclables out Thursday morning, shopping for our weekly groceries early Monday morning just after breakfast. No matter what I do the rest of the day something to get me started early opens up many possibilities for the day ahead. I am more prone to do something physical than to sit down at the computer and surf the hours away.

You must take care of your life. Keep it interesting but stay involved and active. Sitting in the chair and watching the television will only put you in the grave sooner and deny you the opportunity to enjoy this time in your life. You must reprogram yourself, to a new schedule and keep it. If emergencies arise fit each emergency into the existing and possibly ever-changing schedule. This orderliness will give you an overall sense of purpose which should not end with your work life. Remember what my brother told me: if you go out and buy a gallon of milk, that's a pretty good day. And even with a tight schedule, make changes as needed to allow you to honor responsibilities to others and to proclaim a day of recuperation when needed.

VIII

Day to Day

I do not claim to have the only solution to what could be a retirement in which you will have too much time on your hands, nor do I claim that your time will be impossible to manage due to all the thing that time allows you to now do. The orderliness of a day to day approach to retirement will give you the structure that most will miss upon leaving work. You may have never thought about it, but your job was a protection, in a way. For those hours a week for which you were committed in your job, no one could call for immediate help or advice. You were protected from being drawn into something for which you had no time to give. This may be seen as not a good thing. It is, however, a fact, that all that you were to do during working hours was to benefit your boss and not you or a friend in need.

The structure that the job gave you may be the thing that most people miss. It gave a framework of concerns that preempted one's own personal concerns and offered stability that many will not find in retirement. If you need structure do not wait to find out the hard way. Be proactive and set up a regimen for yourself that you can change if you need to, if you find that you need no schedule you will be one of the rare ones. A schedule with times and dates will guard against finding out the hard way that structure is important to you.

As I have suggested keep a calendar that contains all of the appointments and events to which you are committed. It is often the case that the retiree feels that to wear a watch or keep a schedule is to much like work or the deadline mentality of work. You must still meet appointments even if they are solely yours now and not job related. If you need a schedule, you will make a mess of your retirement not keeping up with time and events. My wife keeps a calendar for both of us so that we can know when we have free time together and when we must visit the doctors office or meet some other obligation on time.

I had a friend who retired and organized an early morning breakfast with other retirees in order that his day would get off to a structured start. This is a way to get up and out of bed and start the mind working and the body moving. After breakfast then the appointments and chores can be scheduled before lunch. Having meals and meal times that are fixed, if no special lunch event is planned, will get you through the first half of the day. Some find it important to take a nap, an event that work-a-day people are not used to, but which may proved helpful in keeping up your energy after lunch and can get you ready for the afternoon and evening events. The evening meal may not be something that can be scheduled to include all the family for everyone may not be available. Do what you can to provide the familial contact needed to know what others are doing and a time to tell you family and friends what you are doing and planning. Make sure that your bed times are fairly consistent, or as consistent as possible. Changes in your activity levels and fluctuating bed times may cause you to over sleep or under sleep based on you day's activities. If you play fast and lose with your bed times then the idea of structuring your days may suffer. Even if your schedule calls for late nights and late rising, try to keep the pattern of activities the same and you will probably do much better with your days.

Now there will be those that feel that time weighs heavily on their hands: too many hours each day and relatively little to fill those hours. If your work life had given you only hours to relax afterward and you have developed little to occupy your time, now that it is so abundant, then fill that time with activities that you can enjoy and possibly make money if you need it. If you plan properly the need for more money may be avoided. Do not continue working, unless you must, with the ideas that you are going to add appreciably to you savings. Work is a commitment for which you have to give so much of yourself that the amount that you make in a support position will almost never pay for the wear and tear on you.

Every one will have different needs, but make sure that you have a schedule to fall back on, and, when there are repetitive events in you days, try and standardize them so that you may bring other activities into your schedule without time shuffling.

IX

Finances

If you are fortunate enough not to have ongoing physical problems, finances may prove difficult. If you have both health problems and financial problems each will potentiate the other and finances may be made more difficult having to pay out for doctors, medicines and hospital stays. You should have a "gap policy" that pays what Medicare does not , if you do not have Medicare sign up for it three months before your qualifying birthdate, usually at age 65 or 66. Do not wait on this or signing up for Social Security for it takes months for the government to process you and get you the services that they offer. Next contact your primary work coverage insurance company to make sure that they have the date of your Medicare coverage, when it will replace the work insurance policy as the primary coverage in your retirement. It maybe that you will want another insurance company to be the gap policy to pick up all other payments that Medicare does not pay (the other 20 percent). Also you may want to use your gap insurance to pay for the bulk of you drug bill. Check prices to see whether your work insurers are the cheapest if not try another drug supplying insurer like Cigna, a very cheep and dependable mail order drug supplier. Getting drugs in the mail, over the phone or on line, is more convenient and means that you do not have to go to the drugstore and stand in line, a problem for many of us.

Once you have your Medicare and gap policy set up (Remember Medicare will pay 80 percent and your gap provider will usually pay the other 20 percent), and you have signed up for Social Security, it is time to take care of the day to day expenses. If possible complete all of these signups before you start living the life of a retiree, if you cannot then make sure that you attend to these three signups, Social Security, Medicare and your insurance gap policy as soon as possible.

Do not think that you will be able to live cheaper than you did when you were working, if you do you will find yourself running out of money before more money comes in. With Social Security, Medicare and your gap policy with drug provisions, you are ready to deal with the day to day payments which need to be carefully controlled.

If you have saved money for retirement it may be in a 401(k) or a 403(b) through your employer. These are government mandated in a way that protects your money, but the fact that you may not loose as much over time of the money that you put in, the truth is that you will not see the money you invest grow sufficiently to probably cover all your needs. What your monthly intake of money does not pay, your savings should not fill the gap. This is money for those things that you do not buy everyday like a washing machine or a used car. You must live on the money that comes in regularly. If you do not do this the money that you save, at least that most people save, will not allow you to regularly tap the savings without losing that money that you may need latter in your retirement.

You need, and it is a risky business, to put your money in fairly adventurous investments that will tend to replace in profits, interest and dividends, the monies that have to be take out for emergencies. Also your money should grow beyond what you remove for emergencies several percentage points, three or four percentage points, in order to keep up with inflation which takes the value of your money away each year.

Look at the overall value of your savings. If that amount is not growing above the withdrawals and the inflation rate, then you have not had a good year. The tendency is to put money into accounts where your money or principle cannot be lost. This is a sure way to lose your money. With out a diversified investment strategy you will watch monies that you do not rob beyond replacement be eaten up over time. Find a good dependable investment firm. I do not advise that you use an individual since they can be gone with your money, and you could be broke if he decides to run off with your money to his own retirement. A good company like Fidelity or Vanguard, will be able to closely match your needs with a risk level that you can live with without having sleepless nights for worry. I am not recommending a course of action only the ones that I have taken, and for the time and my situation they have worked out well. If you do lose money with these company for a while, as I have from time to time, they have been shown to rebound very quickly to put you once again on the profit side of investment. Be realistic, you will have periods of loss but the bond and interest markets will never be able to give you the increases in your money that you will probably need unless you have millions of dollars to invest. A good diversified investment strategy can make up in a day the amount of money that an interest bearing account can provide today through fixed interest investments and most dividend paying stocks.

The main warning is to stay within the financial limits that you set for retirement so you have enough money to live and have a savings nest egg for those things that your day to day plan cannot pay for, and never let the savings become the day to day money that you need to make it through each month.

Each year look at your assets and determine whether you met your goals of sustaining your investment funds. It is staggering to image that inflation could over a thirty year retirement for you and you wife could see one thousand dollars, due to inflation, lose its purchasing power and have little more purchasing value than one hundred dollars. Your yearly measure of worth is the best way to give yourself a way to gauge your financial retirement health.

Conclusion

If you have not experienced retirement do not assume that you have all the answers, as I did. With the loss of a work career, there are issues of identity that result from leaving the one thing, that by the amount of time spend in its pursuit, has defined who you are. I did not believe this to be true of myself, but after a few months of retirement and meltdown proved that I was a product of my work life. Thought of work has taken not only your working hours but much of your non-working time. In imbues your life with an outlook that is different because of your job and its responsibility. It has probably controlled our dress, our housing and even the type of cars that we drive. Our work may even determine the type of activities that we are involved in outside of the workplace. There is no way that we can escape the influence that is carried over into our retirement even to our understanding of who we are.

Leaving that job can create a serious void in your life. This can for most be a traumatic time. Do yourself a favor and preplan your entry into retirement. Make the transition smoothly from work to leisure. Provide a guide, a structural plan, a framework into which you can introduce a schedule in order to provide stability to a time that is otherwise unstructured. Oh, you may eat breakfast and other meals at about the same time, but there is much time between meals that need managing. If after several months you do not think that you need to schedule activities in your days, then stop keeping a calendar and let life become one big surprise from day to day.

You may also find that travel, hobbies and random activities will suffice to keep you interested and eager to rise to each new day. This is, as I have examined it, not the reaction of most retirees. I spent about a year and a half traveling only to be glad to remain at home, if for no other reason than the fact that I have my own bed and bath and do not have to live out of a suitcase. Retirees also do not have the physical mobility to sustain long sojourns, and if this is not true now it will probably be a near future concern. The problem that hobbies do not always give a lasting feeling of satisfaction was my next realization.

Make sure if you decide to not provide a calendar of events for structure, that you have the temperament for a loose retirement, where what ever happens happen. If your temperament as in work was a bit tense do not fail to provide a tighter, more active and more productive day, and by all means introduce a formal schedule into your retired life.

A schedule does not mean that you must stick with every thing that has been put into your calendar. When alternative activities arise, by pass the schedule and then return to the schedule when free to do so. Let the schedule take over when there is no emergency or no planned adventure. Give yourself at least a year to work within the schedule. Do not make any major life changing decisions within at least this time frame. You do not know what retirement will be for you in the short term, so save the big decisions for latter when you know a little bit more about you as a retiree and the life that you may have to lead.

Without a plan that is based on your financial situation, there can be no clear road ahead for you. Know what your bills are and how much you will have coming in each month. Allow for budgeting for those long-term expenses like property taxes and any balloon, or escalating, payments that need to be meet within their time frames. If nothing else, write checks that spread the large payments out over their duration. Finally, do not use your savings for everyday needs. Make sure that you are able to get to some money for emergencies as all other monies need to be invested to keep you from reducing your principle, and over come the inflation rate which will eat away your savings. Inflation can cause you to lose money without spending it. And make sure that your savings are growing with any deductions for emergency or infrequent large ticket items.

You will learn how to live in retirement. It could be one of the better experiences in your life, or it may be a frustration and a financially challenging time. Make sure that you are prepared for all the pit falls that could make this time a struggle for you. Your fishing may be important but you do not want to eat fish every night and don't count on selling them to pick up necessary money to get you through your retirement years.